LIVING ABOVE THE FROST LINE
New and Selected Poems

Nancy Simpson

LIVING ABOVE THE FROST LINE
New and Selected Poems

Nancy Simpson

Laureate Series

CAROLINA WREN PRESS
Durham, North Carolina

Editor: Andrea Selch

Design: Lesley Landis Designs
Cover Image: "Misty Mountain" ©1981 A. J. Zimmermacher
Author Photograph: © 2009 Lynn Hamilton Rutherford

The mission of Carolina Wren Press is to seek out, nurture and promote literary work by new and underrepresented writers, including women and people of color.

This is the inaugural book in the new Carolina Wren Press Laureate Series. This publication was made possible by a generous grant from the North Carolina Arts Council. In addition, we are grateful for the ongoing support made possible through gifts to the Durham Arts Council's United Arts Fund.

Library of Congress Cataloguing-in-Publication Data

Simpson, Nancy, 1938-
Living above the frost line : new and selected poems / by Nancy Simpson.
       p. cm.
ISBN 978-0-932112-61-3
I. Title.

PS3619.I56393L58 2010
811'.6--dc22

2010021880

ACKNOWLEDGMENTS

Appreciation to the literary magazines or presses that first
published or reprinted these poems:

From ACROSS WATER

The Art Journal: "Alone on a Mountain in an Unfinished Cabin;"
Georgia Review: "Water on the Highway;" *Kalliope*: "Crowded
House" and "Walking Away;" *Nethula*: "Thoughts of the Fisherman
Walking the Shoreline;" *NewCollAge Magazine*: "Dark Side;"
Tar River Poetry: "The Wreck;" and to the State Street Press for
these and all other poems in this section.

From NIGHT STUDENT

The Arts Journal: "In the Presence of Wegia," "Last Oak in the
Schoolyard," and "Night Student;" *Atlanta Magazine*: "Sharing
the Bed With Mother;" *Collecting Life: Poets on Objects Known
and Imagined*: "The Collection;" *Davidson Miscellany*: "White Lie;"
Florida Review: "For the Set Man;" *Georgia Journal*: "At the End
of the Drought;" *Georgia Review*: "Lives in One Lifetime;" *Indiana
Review*: "Leaving in the Dead of Winter;" *Kalliope*: "Floating"
(Selected by William Stafford as the winner of the Florida Fine
Arts Festival Poetry Contest); *Negative Capability*: "On the River;"
Portfolio: "Foxes;" *Southern Poetry Review*: "The Girl," and "Grass,"
("Grass" was also reprinted in *Southern Poetry Review*'s 50th
Anniversary Issue, *Don't Leave Hungry*, published by University
of Arkansas Press); *Wayah Review*: "On Certain Days of the Year"
(now titled "Heritage"); *Light Year*: "Pink Pantsuit;" *Tar River
Poetry*: "Driven into the Interior;" and to the State Street Press for
these and all other poems in this section.

From **IN THE SOUTHERN MOUNTAINS**
EXCHANGING IDEAS ON THE SUBJECT OF ART

Catalyst: "The Green Girls;" *Confrontation*: "In the Southern
Mountains: Exchanging Ideas on the Subject of Art;" *The Georgia
Journal*: "Accounting," "Frederick at the Piano," "The Language
of Ants" and "Lost Man;" *Lull Water Review*: "Tanfastic;" *New
Virginia Review* (now *Blackbird*): "The Gleaners" and "Network
News;" *South Florida Review*: "The Poet's Voice;" *Wayah Review*:
"Cicadas Returning."

From **LIVING ABOVE THE FROST LINE**

Appalachian Heritage: "At the End of Always;" *Atahita Journal*:
"The Storm;" *Cooweescoowee Journal*: "The Ghost of Candide;"
The Georgia Review: "Transplanting;" *Journal of Kentucky Studies*:
"Teaching Myself How to Burn Last Year's Leaves;" *Pembroke
Poetry Magazine*: "What She Saw and What She Heard;" *The Poets
Guide to the Birds*, Anhinga Press: "Carolina Bluebirds;" *Prairie
Schooner*: "Now in Another Land," "Skin Diver's Memory,"
"Studying Winter," and "Walking Around Lake Knowles with
Sarah."

AUTHOR'S ACKNOWLEDGMENTS

Thank you to Carolina Wren Press for choosing these poems for publication as the first book in the new Laureate Series.

Special appreciation to North Carolina Poet Laureate Emerita Kathryn Stripling Byer for comments and consistent encouragement. I first met her when I invited her many years ago to read her poems at the library in my town. We became lifelong friends. Down through the years she read every poem I have written and has seen every collection I assembled. I can never repay Kathryn Stripling Byer enough. I owe her much for helping me grow as a person.

Judith Kitchen, fellow poet and writer, has been my friend since seems like forever. We met in the M.F.A. writing program and, after graduation, her State Street Press published my early work. I know now that she went before me in airplanes and into English department offices across America, speaking my name, handing out copies of my book, sometimes reading my poems at her own readings. I wish I could repay my debt to her. One of my dearest memories is that she asked me to be best woman at her wedding.

I also owe thanks to Steven Harvey, my poetry mentor, to Bettie M. Sellers, Blanche Farley, and Janice Townley Moore. They were the first poets I met when I began to write in the 1970s. They insisted I study poetry and pointed the way. My appreciation also goes to the N.C. Writers Network West, to both the poetry and the prose monthly critique group members. They are more than associates to me.

Thank you to John C. Campbell Folk School for Writer-in-Residence opportunities.

—Nancy Simpson

Dedicated to My Sons,
Timothy Reid Brantley and
Jeremy Quoc Phong Brantley,

and in memory of Jeffery Taylor Brantley

*"I must study war that my sons may have liberty
to study philosophy in order to give their children
the right to study painting, music, poetry, architecture…"*
—John Adams (1790)

CONTENTS

1994–2009, *Living Above the Frost Line*

FOREWORD

Nancy Simpson has enriched the literary community of North Carolina for over thirty years. Her work was first heralded by the late Richard Hugo when he read and celebrated her poems at the Callanwolde Literary Festival in Atlanta, shortly after she began to show her poetry around to friends and readers in the far reaches of western North Carolina. He praised her rich inner life and her ability to give expression to it as it manifested itself in her everyday life. Whether driving on Standing Indian Mountain in "Night Student," expressing the complexity of self in "Driven into the Interior," or documenting the carnage of the first Gulf War in "Voices from the Fringe," she brings the inner and outer worlds of her experience into a harmony that resonates like the current giving voice and shape to the mountain creeks she loves. Her poetry resonates with the land she lives upon and the memories she carries with her. She is also fiercely engaged in the ethical life of this country, an unswerving pacifist and defender of place and its people. Both plain spoken and lyrical, her poems speak with a voice that knows where it comes from, honoring that place and the web of relationships that exist within it. She can make the world shimmer in a single line. She can break your heart. She can sing. She does what a poet has to do, wake the reader into a fresh vision of reality.

Living Above the Frost Line: New and Selected Poems traces the growth of a poet determined to survive despite the obstacles raised by age, mortality, and the inevitable losses that come from being alive in this world. Through her poetry she greets that half-drowned woman, harking from her Florida girlhood, who appears as her muse in "Bridge On the River Kwai, " bearing gifts of memory and sustaining images. In return the poet gives her "a mountain, the safest place to be." Rarely has the relationship between poet and muse been so beautifully expressed.

I met Nancy in the summer of 1978, when she invited me to read at the Clay County Library. My daughter was only a few months old, and I recall my husband walking her around the town square while I read, so that she would not disturb anyone should she begin to cry. Afterward Nancy and I stayed in close touch, sharing our poems and those of other poets we admired, as well as our desire to help generate a community of writers and readers in our mountain region. Some of her first poems were published in *The Arts Journal,* a monthly publication out of Asheville, for which I was Poetry Editor. Those years were time of transition for her as both poet and woman finding her way beyond the traditional roles of wife and mother. Her love for the western North Carolina landscape began to take metaphorical shape in her poetry, giving voice to the interplay between the human voice and that of the physical world around her.

After receiving her MFA degree from Warren Wilson's low residency program, where she worked with Heather McHugh, her chapbook and a full-length collection were published by State Street Press, edited by Judith Kitchen. A recipient of a North Carolina Arts Council Fellowship, Simpson has published widely in magazines ranging from *The Georgia Review* to *Prairie Schooner,* but her own work soon became secondary to promoting a literary community in the far western area of the state. As a teacher in the Clay County Schools, she came to this calling instinctively, sensing the need for expression in her students' lives. She has devoted numerous hours to mentoring both young and older writers, and finally helping to create what has become Netwest, part of the North Carolina Writers Network. Over the years, she has become the nurturer and cheerleader for countless writers in the western counties, teaching workshops, serving as Writer-in-Residence for the John C. Campbell Folk School, and editing two collections of work by mountain writers.

Living Above the Frost Line richly deserves the honor of being the first collection published in Carolina Wren's Laureate Series. No one better illustrates the gifts that poetry can offer than Nancy Simpson. She has never doubted its power to change lives and awaken our sense of wonder in the midst of the world in which we find ourselves. Brilliant writer, teacher, tireless editor, Nancy Simpson exemplifies the best in our state's literary community.

—Kathryn Stripling Byer,
North Carolina Poet Laureate Emerita

ACROSS WATER

The sun is hot today and my map is marked, open.
I drive home, knowing as I go,
I will have to cross water to get there.

Driven into the Interior

She climbed on spiral stairs
above the city, inside
the skull of a dome,
a girl, alone.
Call it Rite of Passage.
Always afterward she was old.

Reversion is certain,
life so dull at times she turns inward
remembering a bookshelf in the classroom

Geographic Magazine
FOR STUDENTS WHO ARE GOING PLACES

worn cover, same page every time,
the picture of a woman, bare-breasted
lighting a fire.

In the photo she saw The Great Mother,
Queen of Heaven, carved from stone,
her head proud, breasts and hips immense.
She felt a sudden reverence
for the dove carved from soapstone,
womb-shaped, and new respect
for bowls and the oven in her kitchen.

She never went far though, except to Bagdad
in Florida when she was young.
When she grew up she lived in Appalachia,
and she placed on her shelf small offerings,
the shell of a turtle. Many shells.

Walking Away

A girl stomped her feet,
terrified maybe, so she smashed memory
beyond recognition. The closet floor
may still be strewn with sandal straps,
but she stayed plucky. She believed
in trees and dreamed Vizcaya belongs
to everyone. Before you walk away,
let me say she did not float ashore
in a coconut hull as her mother told
but was born the hard way at Homestead:
Born underwater in the Atlantic, drowning
and living, Key West, Miami, Jacksonville,
born in a cornfield one summer in Georgia,
Macon, Atlanta, Dalton, working her way up
into the highlands, old lives thrown down,
dropped like freezing rain on the north ridge
of a Carolina mountain. How many years
has she lived in the shadow on the northside?
Having learned the leaves of trees,
the language of ants, not much scares her.
Driving into the valley she says
she will not climb that mountain again.
Don't believe it. This is true.
She painted the old cabin
and rented it to lovers.
Anemone grows in the window box.
Bloodroot blooms on the path.

Water on the Highway

Water on the pavement moves before me,
Witch Water, I say, as though some sorceress waits
snapping her crooked fingers to make it disappear.
It is real I tell you. It evaporates,
or seems to, and it is always there.

Last night a friend talked about going home,
the roadmap she followed, the bridge she had to cross.
As I listened, I studied her words on paper
describing a house with stained glass windows,
a wicker chair, her father's face. I want to believe
poets who say this is the way home, who go and come
traveling lines as concrete and safe as any interstate.

The sun is hot today and my map is marked, open.
I drive home, knowing as I go,
I will have to cross water to get there.

Bridge on the River Kwai

All those times, all those bridges,
Georgia to Florida, sand
in his shoes, red clay in his pocket,
I wonder what passed through my father's mind.

He never said much about hurricanes
or corn, except that you pull it not pick it.
One summer in Georgia I promised to pull
all the corn in ten acres he planted.

Indolent girl, red clay in my pocket,
I remember a movie in East Atlanta.
Prisoners built a bridge across water,
building, building, the whole movie.

I was too young to know why
they blew it all to pieces in the end.
This morning a half-drowned woman wakes me.
I open the window. She has come many miles

across water. Her memories are mine.
She gives me one starfish, one mango
and reminds me how I climbed the tree
when the flood came, after the hurricane.

I give her anemone for starfish.
I give her a mountain, the safest place to be.

On a Mountain in an Unfinished Cabin

Rafters make a shadow on the wall,
backbone, rib cage.
I have not seen this many shadows
in all my lives put together.
When it is not raining I hear
the forest scream. I dream in color.
Some nights there is blackness
until six in the morning.

Later I wake not knowing it is Monday.
All the trunks are black.
My own grief wraps tight as a vine.
This is the day I begin to talk to myself.
*I did not come here to be stung
by a hornet.* I say this to one
that storms the deck
to eat leftover moth wings.

According to my family I've disappeared.
All of us leave home sometime,
so I exist two weeks on a mountain
with my Norwegian Elkhound. Wegia
speaks. She tells me to bathe,
comb my hair. I know it is time
to walk to the top of the mountain.
This makes me think

I am among the living.
So many trees,
I make an agreement with leaves,
acting silly, singing–
*Give me all your oxygen,
I'll give you CO_2.*
Wegia is pleased. It rains.
We watch the sun set as if visible.

Dark Side

Rain falls on my house
drumming up the old woman in me,
cave woman, afraid in the dark.
Rain makes a wall between earth and sky.
Not one star. *There is no moon*
I say blind in my belief,
but surely there are stars
and the moon is somewhere in the heavens,
stumbling along, shoved along,
pushed over the edge maybe.

The Girl with the Black Innertube

Believing the sun that made me native
has come to save me, I rise and go
half-dressed to hunt for higher ground.
Eight days of rain, and salamanders climb
on the rocks, the stream saturated.

It is possible to come to grips with mushrooms,
to plant sea grapes, palm trees,
to lie back moving mountains beneath me
so I fit like a flock of sea gulls
hearing in the swish of fronds
the going out and coming in of waves.

The girl with my legs drifts
on a rubber tube past breakers,
past jetties. I watch her go,
remembering the taste of salt.
What good it is to walk on the beach
waving a towel, calling *Come here, come home?*

She turns her back to me.
This is the way of girls who dream.

Thoughts of a Fisherman Walking the Shoreline

Whispering yes and yes again in darkness
they came, forty, maybe more,
holding out their hands, saying with one voice,
Here is our money. Sell us your boat.

After war they go, women thirsty for oceans,
men who never studied the logs of the dead;
their children hungry
for sun that shines on water.

I meant to say no, yes, but
hands touched mine, money, warm.
No need for the vessel now anyway.
Two of my sons died in the war. One lives
in the north, not a fisherman by trade.

There are rotten boards on deck
and leaks I should have patched. Why worry?
No one walks the beach looking for bodies.
I buy fish and no one asks
Where is your boat old man?

The Wreck

Witnesses saw it all, heard the crash,
the speeding blue Camaro stopped dead
at Pinelog Bridge. Sam Beck insists
he saw a man fly through the windshield,
careening through air, velocity 100 mph,
maybe more. Searchers dragged the river,
trudged bottomland three days, hunting.
We all stop sooner or later
but something in me wants to know
why they never found him, where he went.
Something in me moving fast
wants to fly out through my eyes
like a body thrown free of the wreck.

Traveling

I think first of my father,
how one day he did not remember
passing through town. Everything
looked different. He guessed
his mind was somewhere else.

I want to thank him
for telling me, so casually he spoke.
I want to thank him,
it means I'm not crazy,
for he was not crazy.
The night he died
he knew what he was doing.

* * * *

He knew how to die.
We said that of my father
and tell the story,
how he sat on the sofa
hardly breathing,
three nights without sleeping.
I was traveling home
from night school in Asheville,
ice on the road in the high elevations.

* * * *

What I know I learned from my mother,
so good she was to tell me
how he sat on the sofa, praying
calling the names of his children.

God is going to let me sleep,
he said, and died within minutes,

at the same time I was dreaming
white cloudlands, white seals,
my car plowing homeward
through Winding Stair Gap.

Crowded House

The young in me are leaving,
a whimper, a tear drifting off
so I assume they take their wounds.
God knows I have taught them and taught them.
I put down my switch to count
which ones are left. Thank goodness

the busy girl is gone, tied up in traction,
a bad back and a hateful disposition.
She never minded a word. *Stand,* I said
but she slumped.

The believer is here part time, a student
inquiring into books stacked to high heaven,
The Apology, Crito, Phaedo. She thinks
truth was written long ago.

The one who loves men left and came home
married and pregnant. Now I am mother-in-law,
and a grandmother to her noisy daughter.

As for the peacemaker, she is going off to war
and has forgotten how our feet pounded the pavement,
how many marches it took to end just one war.

The sensitive one walks on the mountain. I know
how she dreams to get free.
She brings phosphorus and a creek stone,
a salamander crawling in the palm of her hand.
She wants me to like her, and I like her, that one,
keeper of the crowded house.

NIGHT STUDENT

What is it at two minutes past twelve,
this funnel cloud in me, this song of forsythia
makes me stop my car at Shooting Creek
to search above trees
where headlights do not reach?

Lives in One Lifetime

Sometimes you get what you asked for,
to be left alone. All day
not once the sound of a motor,
one sailboat only with a yellow flag waving.

From this shore I see where sky begins,
blue between oaks on top of the ridge.
Across Chatuge, the lake made by man,
a whole mountain rises out of the water.

I have no boat and no way to cross over
this flooded valley except to walk.
Where the road was, my feet can touch asphalt
if I let myself sink.
                         Here the house stood.

There was the roof of the barn, buried forty years.
Rubble from lives in one lifetime passes before me.
This is the end, the new start,

rock I remember, and clay soft beneath my feet.
An old logging road leads me up the mountain
where trees stand apart,
where sky begins.

White Lie

End of May, and we have nothing
better to do than walk on the mountain,
our cardigans closed against the cold.
You cannot take back one lie,
not even white ones, subtle

as berry blossoms beside this path.
I kick a stone and tell you I believe
we will pull free from the brambles.
Old timers call this Blackberry Winter,
a temporary cold spell, quick to pass.

Night Student

It is the first shooting star my eyes have seen
breaking blackness above the university parking lot.
I am impressed with Jones,
the spectacular mark he made on my paper.
I have it beside me two hours from home.

Truth is up there over the steering wheel,
keeping up, 60 mph on Franklin Bypass.
Socrates said so. I would like to ask
the Know-It-All what makes stars break.

I drive slow on Standing Indian Mountain
and count the times Jones asked in class,
Is it logically consistent? Ten.
On the radio, static reception,
Linda Ronstadt is singing about a broken lady
waiting to be mended.

I see my face in the rear-view mirror,
not a wife anymore, not a mother,
a thirty-eight-year-old freshman
chewing left over cheese-crackers
that crumble on my fingers, star showers
into the floorboard.

What was it I saw up there, white against black,
like white hairs in brunette,
like the white line on pavement?

What is it at two minutes past twelve,
this funnel cloud in me, this song of forsythia
makes me stop my car at Shooting Creek
to search in space above trees
where headlights do not reach?

Star, one cut with your sword,
you have sliced the night open for me.

Foxes

The sight of the pair
eating bread crumbs on the lawn
makes me imagine I want you
to come back, stand by me again.

Stunned by their green eyes
I am fooled into thinking
I hear you say, as you said,
In the last days of winter
they hunt together.

They are misplaced, they are starving.
But what power! They change me,
change you 800 miles away, wherever
you are. We are at the window
looking out, married in the agreement
that the free suffer.

Leaving in the Dead of Winter

Ghosts push up through soil, pale mushrooms
and Indian Pipe clusters, the little saints.
Let the land moulder. October, November.
Oaks look finished but they will come back.

Some pretend to be dead and lie morbid
on the ground. Saplings rise from the rot.
At night phosphorus glows
in the heart of the oldest stump.

It is natural to live with decay,
to notice the life of a tree and say we die
many times, mutable, all of us.
Still, one must learn how to act,

when to come, when to go.
Here is a scene. In wintertime
a woman packs to go someplace.
Torn photographs fall to the floor. She sees

herself, and the one man she loved, young.
He looks dependable. Now she smashes a red
crystal bowl, and wants to cut everything.
Wait. This is not the end.

The woman drives away fast,
or take it from this point of view—
leaving Cherry Mountain in the dead of winter
you look up and see a backbone sticking out,

huge curve of the ridgeline
shaped like a great whale beached and dying.
The ground has already stiffened.
No one can live this close to death.

Sharing the Bed with Mother

We make ourselves narrow,
a space no wider than a fist between us.
There are rocks in this mattress or worse.
What we sleep on is what mothers and daughters
always had for a bed, the lies we tell each other.

Her breath is even and cool on my shoulder.
This is where we come when we are old,
after husbands have gone or died.
We share a bed miles from where we started.

Blackness, unfamiliar shapes
and I am almost afraid.
She was a child never afraid.
She built her own traps,
caught rabbits alive to please her mother.

If I move I will touch her.
I stay still and make lists
to catalog the lies I have heard and told.

I see her as a mountain. I am a mountain.
This could go on all night,
my wanting to build a bridge
and tear it down, and build it back again.

I wonder what would happen if we spoke
the truth. Maybe there would be no marriage
in the first place. No daughters.
A woman might stand on a crate, shouting
in the middle of town, or on network television.
Girls would listen. That would be the end of it.

I touch her leg. Her feet are cold.
I imagine what if she never wakes,
and I grieve. There is a green lamp
and drapes a deeper shade of green.

Pass to a Seminole Village

A girl walks back across
Miami River Bridge to what was called
Pirate's Cove. In her pocket is a ticket.
In her hand she holds a ripe sapodilla.

Under the thatched chickee
she watches a woman who combs palm fiber
into strands, without pretense,
and curls the strands on her finger

for dolls' hair. In other huts other women
sew cloth strips into garments,
skirts for their daughters.
In the center of the village, the girl

waits for the hour three times in a day
when a man enters the alligator pit.
If the man is afraid of the lightning
lash tails or the alligator's teeth,

no one knows. He takes the gator
and wrestles it gently, kneels in the sand,
rubbing its stomach until it lies entranced
in the sun. With unassuming eyes he looks

at the girl. Only the grunt of the female
can break the spell of the sleeping animal.
He opens the alligator's snout
and rests his neck on the white teeth.

Grass

We ought to be thankful it grows wild
on road banks, sometimes blond and curled.
It holds earth together and still,
we hear Earth is falling.

Sinkholes in the South swallow cars.
We do not doubt, but can we help wonder
what happens when the bottom drops?
Maybe clumps fall with the Jeep

and the Porsche, forming the shoreline
of a lake in some post suburb.
Grass has a right to be cherished,
Crowning Glory, clipped to perfection.

No matter where we sleep we live
with threat hanging over our lawns.
Who says we need more weapons?
We want to know what will happen to grass,

grass everywhere, amber savannahs,
sacred as the hair on our heads.

Pink Pantsuit

It hangs around the wardrobe
for days, dull,
or reclines in the hamper

like a flattened flamingo.
I wash it in soft water.
I give it new life, and what thanks?

It walks out the door with my legs,
through the gate,
headed straight for the racetrack.

For the Set Man: Clyde Simpson

Mosquito Hell you named the place,
marshland on Biscayne Bay. We found
a boathouse nearly overgrown,
a marble pool on the rooftop,
sunken bath of the very rich. You said
it was the perfect place to find Gatsby.

It was
        a day so clear. I remember Vizcaya,
where movie stars came for parties.
You thought we had light, one hour maybe
to find our way along the shore.

Sundown caught us, Brother. Halfway around
ten million bloodsuckers came after us.
We slapped our own faces.
                        Our feet sinking in mud,
we ran the best we could to your old Buick,
me squalling like Margaret O'Brien
and you saying I should be on the stage;
I knew how to bring on the tears.
That made me uncertain. I have forgotten
how to act.
        When Father died
I phoned the sheriff, nonchalant,
but what do I do now—with you
in that Mosquito Hell Hospital—cry, not cry,
stand by the telephone, my face painted?

On the River

I admit my perception was warped
when I saw the sun floating
large as our small boat.
And when I saw my own soul—
a dark-shaped woman reaching
across the drifting sun—
it was a figment, sun-blindness
from watching my mother-in-law
casting over the water.
It seems right to imagine her

still fishing in Florida,
agile and leaning over the water.
But she is not agile.
I have not seen her for seven years.
For that matter, she is no longer
my mother-in-law. Now
when the sun stays behind clouds
and she cannot go in the boat,
I remind myself that being logical
with the past changes nothing.

Floating

Hovering over the kitchen table
she saw her body sitting on a chair,
intended to stay
                    forever split,

born that second,
3:30 in the afternoon.

Half heard, rattle of the school bus,
dust from Crow Valley Road sifted in
through window screen
                         small worlds floating,

settling on the table, on the window sill.
This one came from a woman who died in 1865.
This one has oceans to be sucked up by sun.

She counted grains of Georgia dust that day,
brain friable in small thought. I know her,

how she saw through screen, a needlepoint picture,
her sons carrying books, climbing the hill.

Last Oak in the Schoolyard

The oak died the day they poured
hot asphalt over its roots.
I mark report cards and watch
men working in rain, all day
the buzzing of their chain saw.
It is the wheeze of emphysema
killing my father. It is his snore.

It is the roar of a motorcycle
topping the hill on a blind trail,
a crash. The tree falls.

All day, an ax hacked.
I have no stomach for dismemberment.
Becky Ledford, Teacher of the Year,
raps three times on glass.
I open the window. She is crying.
At 3:30 I walk past men loading firewood
onto a black pickup truck.
Schoolchildren will pound
chalk dust from erasers
on the stump.

The Girl

I blame her for everything that touches ground,
the girl who throws books and scissors
and screams for no reason
except language will not work for her.
She pulled a fistful of my hair.
She broke my glasses. My back hurts
from lifting her into her wheelchair or desk.

At the school this morning
day was lit with green fog and I half hoped
air on the move would take me ten thousand miles.
I hoped I could teach her something,
the girl who never controlled one thing in her life
but controls me.
                    I slam the door of my own house.

Leaves curl on the forest floor like wrens.
My mind must collect itself.
I screamed for no reason
and have come to sit on a stone. At sundown
mountains are purple with rage
and birds are falling from a sourwood tree,
red bird, red bird, yellow one.
I am going to sit here until someone tells me different,
afraid everything is going to fall,
berries from dogwood, hickory nuts,
every leaf on every tree, and rain.

Heritage

Sun and moon at the same time,
my boy looks up saying Carolina sky
is different from sky in Vietnam.
Nguyen Quoc Phong, Nguyen Quoc Phong,
he writes his name on the fogged windshield.
The anniversary of adoption, he asks

too many questions. I am trying to explain
day and night. We are somewhere between
home and his dad's new house,
coconut cake on the back seat
and presents tied with white ribbon.
But that is not enough.

He wants to know how separate worlds revolve,
the crossing of paths on certain days of the year.
I apologize, driving us south,
remembering the day I reached halfway
around the world, $1600 in my fist,
believing I could give him the sun and the moon.

The Collection

For a long time you collected the dead,
jay feather, bear claw. Even now in a box,
tail of a squirrel, shell of a snail.

But relics do not interest your son.
He is suspicious. What kind of mother
would want to keep sharks' teeth
found long ago in shallow water?
He is alive and running
ahead of you on the mountain.
His dog is his shadow.

September, green going slowly back to yellow,
you want to pick for him one twig of maple,
let him hold one two-colored leaf.
It is too late. He tells you
yellow will come precisely on October 15th,
too many days at a desk, five autumns
with the science teacher
pressing leaves on wax pages.

What can you give the boy this second?
He seems determined to run,
climbing on stones where you cannot follow.
Stop. Wait a minute! No. He turns his back
to you and the spring branch,
diverts his eye from the rock shelf
where thin shells of crawfish gleam underwater.

Leaves argue retirement. Some of them fall
on the path as you walk toward home.
Bones don't know anything, he vows.
You give him your word. You promise
to think more of the living.

Circus World Woman: Irma Crystal

She hangs by her long black hair
twirling her body wild as a wasp
in the top of the tent. We roar
our capricious cheers and applaud her.

A single plume floats down.
We could grow sad watching it descend
to the grass. Tonight
we suspend our disbelief.

Her feathered cloak drops to the ground,
and we see she is a teaser. She strips
and tosses her spangled gown. She flies.
Now, high in the air a guy wire holds her taut.

She is juggling fire on white sticks
as we sit tight on rickety bleachers,
believing as when we were young
if she drops one torch the whole world will burn.

Small Scope

I know asphalt spreads
and pavement exists. Everywhere
the natural world is diminished.
If I have grandchildren they
may never see a squirrel. Still
I believe creatures live in the woods
near my house. Every day or two
a skunk leaves its carcass on the road
as it crosses over to drink in Lake Chatuge.
Today I park on blacktop at Chatuge Shores

and walk across sand with my shoes on.
After a while, seeing no one,
I take off my shoes and wade.
For the first time in the middle of my life
I come to see nature in small scope.
Of all things, here is a spider
with long legs walking on water.
I need to gain perspective. I am trying
to see myself, though
it would be easier to see into asphalt.

Leaves loll on the trees.
Everywhere I witness
branches lifting their pale tongues.
Dust cakes on stumps. Leaves yellow
and trees go blank. Old-timers say
It is too soon. Men walked on the moon,
messed up the weather. They say
Where is our water, our drizzle?
It must be raining in the desert.
Men walk on the moon and earth

grows small. Looking back
I see earth. I see myself
and all of us, minute.

At the End of the Drought

The artificial daisy in the yard
next door spins on its metal stem
and a steady wind brings rain.

The man in the house
is looking out his window.
He is swaying. Showers come

and every blade of grass falls
in love with water.
What would it be like to feel the wet

drenching my hair, washing my back?
I would be a frog leaping:
I would be a duck although

I see this is not a shower.
The opposite of drought is deluge.
The man is dancing half-dressed

under his carport. Now nude
beside the stone birdbath
he is washing his body in the rain.

Skin Underwater

1.
From the top of the mountain we see
Town Valley submerged in clouds.
You say the word *ocean* and a gull
flies from the branch of an oak,
squawks his squawk.

I know a lie when I see one.
Seagulls do live in these mountains.
This is the woodpecker men call extinct,
alive, soaring above oak tops.

Now driving through fog in the valley
you show me things not seen before.
Men are swimming on the courthouse lawn.
Women stare fish-eyed from their gardens,
their mouths turned up.

2.
Barnacles collect on the pier.
Count one for every life you were young:
the schoolgirl, mute,
who spoke only underwater

hoping no one could decipher.
In water memories converge.
Shell is sharp to touch.
Seaweed is soft as hair, and skin

is the large sensor. Skin
keeps its own record of the day
you slit your forearm, diving
into green ocean at South Beach.

Look how barnacles bashed by waves
hold on. Some are encased in stone.
They could cut you bloody, Girl.

3.
Looking back I see my mother
was misinformed, promised an abortion
though it was illegal, five doctors

dead sure I was damaged, and certain
she would die if she gave birth.
She did sort of die, seeing me hideous

in her dream, seeing a ball of hair
bouncing in the room, in the afternoon
when she tried to rest.

I heard from her lips
how she fell down praying.
My mother was devout. I knew
she could not kill. Don't you see?
I was in the best possible position.

4. A voice from a dream

Sleep again.

Dream yourself
on the north bank of the river
inconspicuous as deadwood.

Drift ashore
where grass glows at sunrise,
where light is found all day.

Dream a new body.
a blue robe, and you
walking home.

5.
We stand over the carcass of a jellyfish.
It has given up the ghost, grown opaque.
Moon Jelly, I say, we knew you when
you lit the sky of the underworld.
And we count out loud lines on its body
as if in counting we might learn
how long it lived in the ocean.

Gulls show interest in our arithmetic.
They circle. They fly down
to the sound of our voices.
Are we going to reach the end
of the island? Are we moving in a circle?
Light-headed we walk.

6.
It interests me seeing
the hermit scuttle away
with a moon shell for a new house.

Look how furrows of silt create
a frontal lobe. We are walking,
don't you think, on gray matter?
I will always say yes

to almost everything you ask. *Yes,*
it is possible to imagine
intelligence beneath our feet.

7.
Evening turns out just as imagined.
We walk the length of the beach
and lie on the sand. We enter

the surf, our bodies submerging.
In hearing distance of a wave's yes,
earth is a woman with plans.

IN THE SOUTHERN MOUNTAINS
EXCHANGING IDEAS
ON THE SUBJECT OF ART

*The old bear is gone
and squirrels are settling down-ridge.*

The Gleaners

In the last days of the age
word went out that women
therefore must be allowed
to participate in creation.
And there came forth an artist
calling to us, *Come hither!*

In the center of a cornfield
in Brasstown Valley,
she sculpted an assembly
of corn women. She fashioned
husk bodies, worked six days
making them in her image. She dressed

the corn women in gauze gowns
and entwined eglantine in their
cornsilk hair. *Come hither!*
We entered the cornfield,
our capes waving
in the evening breeze. We

circled the corn women,
lit a circle of small fires
and danced in firelight.
In the morning we came forth
to sculpt, to paint, and to write
the story that is left to tell.

Map

Going home, the road I travel changes
  from four lanes to two.
  from two lanes of pavement to gravel.

The sign: Old Cherry Mountain Trail,
  marks a wagon path used by the Cherokee,
  dirt with ruts.

I trust this road, for I know my way
  with my eyes shut,
  with or without a map.

It's a rough road,
  two way traffic on one lane.
  Slow. Slow.

To know the map inside me
  is to know the name of the first town,
  the name of the first river that flowed.

To know this map is to know
  the first face. Since Day One,
  how many places, neighbors, faces?

Sixty years, some sixty billion faces later,
  do I know anything more than my mother's face,
  looking at me from my rear view mirror?

Argument with My Mother

It was always clear to me
my mother would not lose.
No ambition, she said.
Don't marry that boy,
but I did and when he left
twenty years later, she said, *I told you.*

After Father died, we lived in the same house
and could argue every day if we wanted.
We discussed Magdalene's discipleship,
and debated topics as mundane as seasons.
Mother liked springtime. My passion
was the psychedelia of scarlet maples

flashing on the mountainsides.
I scanned leaves from the poplar's
first yellow glint to golden peak.
She moped saying, *I don't like fall.*
Trees are shedding tears.
In October, each year, to persuade,

I drove her across Chunky Gal Mountain.
I commanded my mother to close her eyes,
so under her eyelids red and yellow pulsed
like strobe lights. She giggled and yielded,
saying *Fall was never more vivid.*
I sighed, and for a while I thought I had won,

but she was right, even if it took her whole life.
When we reached home, she said again,
I don't like fall. It's sad.
Now driving from her funeral
through highlands of sienna and burnt umber,
I concede,
her words on my lips.

The Language of Ants

The girl heard staccato
in segmented syllables.
It scared her—small sounds

under her blanket
spread on the ground,
a chant coming up

through the soil,
thorough grass, through wool cloth,
through her jaw,

a work-song of insects
that build pyramids
and tunnel roads through skulls.

The language of ants
does not carry
a message of resurrection.

She learned
as a child playing with
her doll on the ground

but understands only now,
a woman walking alone
in a field of hills.

Grief Loses Its Grip

First crooked smile,
a giggle, then there comes the urge
to utter words, *I'm back.*
One laugh emits so strangely
it almost hurts, a horse laugh.
When was it I changed direction,
turned around? Yesterday,
a serene smile and humming
as I drove to the store for bread.

The absence of sorrow feels best
in winter, on the first day of a new year.
Joy. The mundane dead.
A friend arrives with news. I learn
all I missed. We drive through the valley,
looking up, nearly ecstatic,
my laughter resounding in witness to
a violet splash, sunlight streaming
across purple mountains near home.

From the Top of the Mountain

in memory of Barbara Simpson Askew

Against my will the Everglades burn.
Smoke blows through the portico
and heat filters in through the window screen.
That was the scene the day you started
to die, Sister, and why I say no
to a road, a highway so humid
and long, it took a lifetime to leave.

I tried comparing the sentimental
and the real, but I don't know
what happened. Proximity is my problem.
If we talked, sipping coffee, saying
what humidity is like, thick air, unmerciful heat,
maybe I could remember more.
Perspective comes from being high,

looking as far into blackness
as my eyes can see, so I rise,
years, miles, reduce the volume
of your wheeze,
erase the whole neighborhood
the day men spread shells on our sand road,
forget they covered every shell with tar.

I only want to remember the last time
you came to my place for a visit.
New Year's Eve. Our party lasted
until Monday, enough snow to cover the leaves.
You laughed at me, a flatlander come to live
on a mountain, how I moved up, teased me
in your girl voice asking, *How high are we?*

Lost Man

The stewardess is still
shaken, and so cold
she cannot describe
the man who stood with her
on the wing of the plane
before it sank into the river.

Divers brought up
from the icy water
the black box
with the pilot's voice.
Soon they will tell us
the last word, why

Flight 90 crashed.
But we may never know
the name of the man
who gave the rescue rope
each time to someone else
until it was too late

to save himself. Who can
tell his name? We only know
when the rescue team came
to lift him from the wing tip
of the plane, he was not there.

In the Southern Mountains:
Exchanging Ideas on the Subject of Art
Dedicated to Alex J. Zimmermacher

When you were six
you sculpted a car
in the sand at Sheepshead Bay
and sat in the car seat for hours.
You say you were nothing
when you were young. You were
a lifeguard, a bouncer,
a government worker. You were
the owner of a shop in Shoreham,
Long Island, a husband, a father,
and later in Florida, an architect.

Now you know me, you say,
but I have trouble
remembering my own lives.
I do not want to know
the date of your birth
nor names of boys
in your old neighborhood, that
your father, who took you to museums,
was a Chicago Opera House clown.
In Yorkville in the 1930s
your sister's paintings burned.

I cannot collect your thoughts.
There isn't room in my head
for your people. Your mother
who made music is dead. Your sister
who never meant to take from you
is schizophrenic in Kansas.
She will not paint.
What do you think? You ask
and say without resentment

she studied at art school
while you had to work.

It's what you do not tell
that makes me listen.
You chose seclusion, came to live
in the mountains. You taught yourself.
Copies of Titian and Renoir
hang on the wall of your studio.
New work, a canvas of waves waits
on the easel, and in your cottage
ink drawings and oil paintings
hang on every wall.
Your mother never saw one of them.

As for me, I like being in a house
where life has to do with art.
And now you know me better,
you say. Our book for today is Marsh,
large and heavy. It collects scenes
of Reginald Marsh from the '30s
and '40s, some from the '50s,
every page crowded as NYC itself,
each painting a congregate of figures.
This is my early life, you say,
lifting the book into my arms.

Network News

My gods are male and female,
small. They are no larger than
a molecule. I don't see
how they got in my blood
but they did. In small ships
they travel with great pomp
through my body. No matter
where they go I get a feeling
they are worshiped. My gods
never fight. They make love
every chance. They get
separated sometimes
when one is sailing
and the other is in port.
They keep in touch,

communicate through a system
I do not pretend to understand.
What good are gods? My friend asks,
my friend who does not believe.
I get embarrassed and feel foolish
for keeping ancient hope.
I know I could go crazy in this
ridiculous world of matter,
everything determined to be physical.
My corn-shuck angel wants to be adored,
and when I look at my bookshelf
a conch shell large as my head
stands where a good book
ought to be. I say to my friend,
We cannot run out of petroleum

soon enough. He shakes his head,
and I shout. *Too many milk jugs
are empty! We will bury ourselves
under plastic.* He goes home,

leaves my logic. Tonight,
even silk roses offend, crowding
my room. I'm distracted
by the commentator's voice
on the ten o'clock news.
Would it be better to turn off
the set, refuse to hear, maybe
make up a lie or two of my own?
I have to make myself laugh
sometimes or go mad
and my gods help me do that.

Cicadas Returning

My neighbor waits
at the mailbox

for no other reason
than to tell me

they are back now
screaming *Pharaoh, Pharaoh.*

He asks if I know
they speak

a language of resurrection.
I say I don't know anything

about cicadas except
I've read they live

most of their lives
under the ground.

He says I should stop
at the switchback

if I want to hear them.
I thank him for telling me.

* * * *

But I care little
about insects,

so I stop against my will,
turn off the truck motor

and stand alone on the
lower mountain curve, listening,

curious about any creature dead
all those years with so much life.

Ten thousand of the little
big-eyed gods crowd my day,

joyous at high pitch:
Pharaoh, Pharaoh.

There will be none homeless
and plenty of food for all—

the lush green leaves of my trees,
enough to feed an army.

* * * *

Come to their senses
they fly

       Cicadae
       Cicadae

their small stomachs
throbbing

       again and again
       the same verse

ten thousand voices
returning, yes

memory of the song
played for me

rising
through treetops

and I am going
down the road, singing.

Walking Up with a Friend

Our path—a crushed-rock road
loops the mountain
designed by developers.
This could depress us
but today we lift ourselves
on our legs, rise above
tree stumps and cabins,
above rooftops and steeples
until we are in the middle
of a lush deciduous forest,
eye level and confronting
the overpopulation of leaves.

We take for our topic
the underside of logic
and keep moving
up the steep side.
When you say, *Starting uphill*
will bring us home
on the downhill climb,
I'm delighted,
pleased to know you
have not dismissed reason.
Yes, you insist, *We are*
going to make sense.

Up is the over side of down.
We are walking across
the high ridge, 2300 feet
in elevation, and now you laugh
because both of us remember
the old quarrel, 2300 feet
is only a hill. Still
we are naturally elated—
It is not every day of the week
friends find time to spend.

We are loquacious as we climb
and soon we are out of breath.
We have come to verify,
to take into account
a mountain we would know blind
from nights we climbed to the top
with a flashlight and lantern.
Today we count ourselves lucky
to gaze long and close
at poplar, oak, chestnut oak.
Their numbers add up.
See how they glow
filled with sunlight, turning
waxed leaves toward us.

As we turn for home,
I forget where we came from.
Through logic I know a highway
winds below in the valley.
I have been there,
and, with a good ear,
hear the drone of a truck
moving north toward town.
We are on the other side now,
held in abeyance by a great
leaf wall, every shade of green
we can imagine.

Accounting

The green ghost in me is the land
I sold to developers.
They wanted money. I wanted time
that money can buy, but got
a kind of poverty. They cut trees,
dug deep septic tanks, and paved
a road across the highest ridge.
I sold my spring branch,
gave up my bloodroot.
Barking dogs frighten fox kits,
the old bear is gone,
and squirrels are settling down-ridge.
Twenty houses line the mountain top
where trees stood. Men who live
in the houses take out their trash,
bring in wood for their fires.
In summer women sunbathe on wide decks
extending out over the mountainsides.
They feel transcendent, viewing
the blue lake that glistens in the distance.
They are exalted looking down on
the slow mob that moves through the valley.
I have some money now
but live with a green ghost in me.

The Green Girls

A young woman with pale lips
sulks under a mimosa tree
holding knees close to her breast.
She does not wave at me today
as I drive past. I know why
or think I know, having seen
her sister walking on the road,
head down, tears on her face.
Why have they quarreled?
One is not lovelier than the other.
Both are smart. I heard
their teacher say one could run
a corporation. The other
might be governor someday.

Mimosa is not Poinciana
though there is relation in the shape
of leaves that never grow larger
than the size of fingernails.
These sisters have power.
They turn back my seasons. I sit
with my back against the trunk
of an old tree, raucous with blooms,
myself young and growing. Poinciana
leaves in profusion turn yellow
and shed, painting my old home
front steps in sunny pointillism.
Mother appears, still sweeping,
still trying to remove the stain.

More lasting than a painting
my sister comes out of the house.
She slams the door, her anger
as vivid to me now as it was.
I want to tell the Green Girls
they will forget why they quarreled.

When they ask their mother, she'll say
she doesn't remember or will blame it
on the tree's inordinate shedding.
I want to tell them the word *despise*
is sometimes used loosely among the young,
assure them the kinship of sisters
transcends roots, trunk, and crown
of almost any trees that grows.

Tanfastic

At 12:17 this Sunday
he is uninhibited
in front of God and
everybody traveling
I-75 South, a man
lounging in the bed
of his red pickup truck.
He is getting his tan
the fast way, 80 mph
stretched out
on his chaise lounge,
his black bikini
drawing the sun down.
He is holding a blue
tumbler in his hand.
I can only guess
what he is drinking.
I want to make a pass,
I mean, get past him
in this god-awful traffic.
I want to see
the face of the woman
at the steering wheel
who is taking him for a ride.

Voices from the Fringe

I. Summer

The surface is hot sand. My level
of endurance seems less than
the woman's in the pink suit
with the black kite on the beach
this noon sunbathing. I saw her
stealth-winged kite flying
this morning when I spread my towel.
My tolerance for heat and sand
will not match her grit. I'm going
into my air-conditioned hotel room
and sit where it's cool. I'm going
back to memory of oak and pine,
myself walking on the forest path.
The understory is a green awning.
Trees are the greatest living things.
I've come to believe my willfulness
derives from their thick trunks,
my tenacity comes from their roots

Armies of nations amass in Arabia
says the radio announcer
between music by Mozart and Haydn.
Saddam Hussein invaded Kuwait
and will not withdraw his troops.
I hear the voice of President Bush
say, *We have masks to protect against*
poison gas. We have to have staying power.
This news makes my drive home
long, nine hours from the coast
to the Carolina mountains.

I don't want my holiday to end
with hostages held as human shields
and soldiers dying in the desert.
Who wants war?
I've only just started to stop
grieving over the last one.

II. Fall

Outside my window
rain lashes the last red leaf
from the sourwood tree.
It's just me and the TV's war talk.
I'm hooked by voices: a woman shouting,
a man sobbing, a soldier saying
            Sand in my bunk, sand in my gun,
            words of a mother asking, *Am I ready*
            to send my son? and the voice
            of President George Bush saying,
            We are dealing with Hitler revisited.

Images lure me to the television,
to satellite News One Feed.
I can't push myself away
from the Saudi Pool Feed
with footage of maneuvers—
a soldier crawls in a trench.
a camel races across the desert.

Videotape 2.
The U.N. permits force.
Congress debates and votes yes to war.
Peacemakers speak. They beat
the peace drum day and night
outside the president's window.

Outside my window—rain, rain.
Saddam Hussein freed the hostages
in Iraq and Kuwait. Into my room
a man is shouting,
        I'm free!
Baker is talking to Aziz.

TV Baghdad. People walk in the streets
waving, shouting. I capture the voice
of an Iraqi woman.
        I hope there will be peace not war.

        III. Winter

Live on World News Tonight with Peter Jennings
it's Gary Shepard in Baghdad saying:
        I'm looking directly west
        of the Al Rasheed Hotel.
        Throughout the entire sky,
        flashes of light, antiaircraft fire,
        a couple of flashes on the horizon.
        Something is underway.

        Peter Jennings says,
        For those just joining us,
        the war has begun.
        American aircraft, perhaps
        American missiles, perhaps
        a Tomahawk fired
        from the Persian Gulf,
        suddenly descended upon Iraq
        and upon occupied Kuwait.
        What was known for so long
        as Desert Shield is now being
        called by President Bush, Desert Storm.

Desert Storm blows across
ancient Mesopotamia and the sands of Arabia.
Flaming debris falls on Israel. The first casualty
is an old woman, gas-mask suffocation.
I know I can't stop this war, barely sleep,
and when I do, I dream of corpses
in chemical suits, face-up on the sand.

Children. Saturday morning.
I turn on the TV to make Tape Number 8.
Peter Jennings walks across a large map,
talks to children sitting at the edge
of the Middle East. A cameraman kneels on Kuwait
waiting as I wait to hear questions children ask:

> *Is the soldier afraid to die?*

> *Why they fighting? Is it for oil?*

> *How long will the war go on?*

> *I want my daddy to come home.*

> *What is a sortie?*

> *What does it mean to visit the target?*

Who can explain to children and other living things
the oil slick 30 miles long, on fire and floating
away from the Ahmade Sea Island Terminal,
away from bombed, leaking oil tankers?
Protesters march in Washington
this cold Saturday. Veterans sing,
> *Hey Uncle Sam. We remember Vitenam.*
> Randy King speaks his belief, a liturgy:
> *I've been through the system.*

I've been used by the system.
I've been abused by the system.
I don't want to see it happen.

Safe in my home I sip tea
and read words on banners
protesters carry:
>   *THOU SHALT NOT KILL.*
>   *BREAD NOT BOMBS.*

I'm tortured by words
of POW Lt. Jeffery Zahn saying:
>   *Our country was wrong to bomb*
>   *the peaceful people of Iraq.*
He was beaten. I am certain.

General Norman Schwarzkopf:
>   *We are softening the battlefield.*
>   *Iraq is a target-rich environment.*
>   *We have flown 10,000 sorties.*
>   *We have air superiority.*

Some neighbors fly the American flag and tie
colored streamers to their car aerial tips.
They tie yellow ribbons around white columns,
believing a ribbon has power
to bring their loved ones home.
In the 5th week of allied bombings,
I rewind, replay Tape Number 11 and see bodies
carried out of rubble. I hear screams
of a father who found his child.

On *Face the Nation* I hear,
>   *The ground war could start at any time.*
>   *The ground war should be avoided.*

SCUDS hit Tel Aviv.
Arabs on the West Bank vibrate their tongues.
I replay tapes, erase parts by mistake.
Some images stay seared in memory.
Isaac Stern plays the violin in concert,
each face before him wearing a gas mask.

The Pool Feed shows American tanks
rolling across sand berms.
> *Iraqi soldiers set 200 derricks blazing*
> *in the Greater Burgan Oil Fields of Kuwait.*

Pool reporters chase the network story.
Mike Vom Fremd corners a pilot
in her Chinook helicopter,
an interview: Sergeant Marie Rossi:
> *To be in any war is an accomplishment.*
> *Sometimes I have to dissociate how I feel*
> *about the prospect of going to war*
> *and seeing the death that is going to be there...,*

(Marie stops, a long pause, stares to the left.)

> *but, as an aviator and a soldier*
> *this is the moment I've trained for.*
> *I am ready to meet the challenge.*

Today President Bush wants us to pray.

> Killed in Action:
> Pfc. Dion Stephenson
> Pfc. Scott Schroeder
> Cpl. Ismael Cotto
> Lance Cpl. James Lumpkins
> Lance Cpl. Eliseo Felix
> Lance Cpl. Thomas Jenkins

Lane Cpl. Frank Allen
Cpl. Stephen Bentzlin
Sergeant Garrett Mongrella
Lance Cpt. David Snyder
Lance Cpl. Michael Linderman, Jr.

I make Tape Number 15.

We have captured 5,000 POWs

We have captured 12,000 POWs

*There is a major tank battle occurring
north of Kuwait City.*

600 oil wells are burning.

25,000 Iraqis surrendered.

In Baghdad all day it's been dark.
People think the bad air has to do with the war.
One said:
      Dark skies for dark days.

40,000 Iraqis have surrendered.

Kuwait looks like Dante's Inferno.

*The greatest battle of the war
is being fought now in Basra.*

Tonight it's network reruns,
so I find and tape film footage
from the Saudi Pool Feed. Not many see this:
the wounded and dead laid on the sand,
moved by helicopter to a tent hospital.

A medic does his work.
The pool feed banner covers
the faces of the dead.

One image keeps me from sleep,
endless lines of surrendering Iraqis,
some crying, some hungry, ashamed
or relieved, one grateful,
kissing his captor.
Who can explain it? They lost
their will to fight. They did not want to die.

In eerie blue footage lit with a night scope,
Forrest Sawyer says Kuwait is a ghost town
and speaks of a fight at Kuwait Airport.

I call the principal of my school.
I can't teach. It seems important
to get the end of the war on tape.
General Colin Powell:
> The Iraqi Army retreats
> under heavy Allied attacks.

President George H.W. Bush:
> We will continue to prosecute the war
> with determined intensity.

Iraq's rout from Kuwait looks like Hell—
a graveyard of tanks,
charred bodies of the dead,
bus loads of bodies, truck loads.

This morning Forrest Sawyer tells a different story.
Kuwait is not deserted.
Kuwaitis stream out of their homes into sunlight.
Says one man:

We were here for seven months like died people.
Now we are in the new life.
Liberation. I listen to natural sound and byte,
the long cavalcade of cars and trucks
filled with men, women and children.
Horns honk. A man blows kisses.
Long live America, America our friend!
My tape recorder failed
with voice only, a black screen,
a segment titled "Letter from Baghdad."
Out of the box a woman's voice is saying:
Our country is sad.
We don't know what will happen.
We're back centuries.
We lost everything.
We lost our future and our past.

IV. Spring

This morning I wake in a different world.
Dogwood trees bloom in the alley
and on mountainsides. What happened to winter?
I don't remember. I sit here at the end of a war.
My friends call. They say *Stop*
watching the tapes. If I could stop, I would.
Fast forward. Rewind.

I pause on the strong voice of Sergeant Marie Rossi—
now dead—and freeze her words,
her pause mid-sentence when she speaks
of death she will see. This war
is over, but not for me. I record scenes
of refugees huddled around campfires,
tape the frightened, starving faces of Kurds,
dying at the border in cold, mountain mud.

It is 98 degrees in May in the southern mountains.
We have humidity that makes me steam,
makes me hold my palm out saying *Stay away.*
My friends visit anyway. *They say, Forget it.*
Memorial Day, I'm still listening.

> *She said, Mom, I don't want*
> *you to worry about me being here.*

> *He said, Well Mom, I've got to go.*
> *I love you, Mom. That was*
> *the last I heard from him.*

My last tape has happy scenes
of soldiers returning home.
On TV troops march
down through the Canyon of Heroes
in lower Manhattan, the Mother of Parades,
commemoration lasting four hours,
cacophony raised to frenzied pitch:
> *U.S.A.! U.S.A.!*
an indelible ostentation,
with ticker tape falling,
and 10,000 pounds of confetti flecking the sky.

Frederick at the Piano

for Janice Townley Moore

You know you are going to find
the audience swollen to capacity
in the community auditorium
at John C. Campbell Folk School.

Isn't it true, there is more in a day
when it rains. Get your boots
and wear the hooded coat.
There is more in a day when

puddles steep the driveway ruts.
Windshield wipers rise. They move.
Count two and keep driving
passed Brasstown Creek out of its banks,

through Brasstown Valley greening.
When you arrive at the concert
in Keith House, there will not be a chair
for you, not even a wooden bench.

Lean against the wall. Listen.
Arpeggios are amplified.
If you want amplitude, look at the piano,
Frederick has four hands.

The Poet's Voice

for Blanche Flanders Farley

What made us drive toward the sun
for three hours, Friend,
facing the glaring Atlanta skyline:
red fireball there then gone,
its flame dispersed on the horizon,
giving us the thought of sky burning?
A poet will read at Emory University
in White Hall. We are going to hear him.

We know his poems and honors received,
hope to see how he takes possession
with words, how he consumes hen, bear.
We are going to lift the poet's voice
from the printed page of his book,
as though *poetry is a wasted breath.*
But look. We might not get there
if the clock tells time. We wandered,

stayed late at a wayside restaurant,
ate slowly, talked thoroughly
about our ordinary lives.
Now, at the entrance, a police car blocks our way.
There was an accident, a student died.
If we want to hear the poet, we must
find another way to White Hall.
We arrive late, stand with others in back.

The man is reciting his famous poem:
The *chilly enduring odor of bear*
rises in the warm auditorium.
He asks for water to drink.
We wait while someone brings
a glass to the podium. The glass
sparkles in his hand.
Soon we are welcomed by his words:

Come in. Sit on a stage step.
There are a few empty seats.
He holds up a copy of his new
Pawtucket poem with its many revisions,
too marked, too long to recite.
He squints as he reads it.
The short Nagasaki poem
he worked for on three years interests me.

I remember Nagasaki bombed,
and I think of driving with you into Atlanta
this evening. *The sky is on fire,* you said.
That red horizon stuns me still,
and I know I came here for no other reason
than to hear the poet, aside, saying:
My friends want to live.
I want to live.

LIVING ABOVE THE FROST LINE

*From my deck, I smell trees
and I am filled with wealth.*

Living on the Mountain

Old trees like old money
smell of richness;
It's not their crowns
that make them regal.
Whether they bow or stand tall,
they do so with a dignity
that can't be bought.
These woods belong to me,
every maple and oak.
How many women do you know
who own a forest?
From my deck, I smell trees
and I am filled with wealth.
Old trees bend. Like women,
like men, they die and fall,
or else they fall and die.
Young ones rise. I love watching
them grow and make their stand.

At the End of Always

Always, you said and I repeated
the word. We could not drink wine
or talk of life until we said it.
Now I sit at your bedside. You don't speak.
I say words you like to hear
and name paintings you forget you painted:
Misty Mountain, Mountain Road,
Yellow Trees. You squeeze my hand,
but you don't open your eyes.
Last Sunday you sat on a chair.
You didn't recognize me. Your glare
pierced straight though my heart.
Today, when I sing, *Hello,*
you know my voice and point
your finger to your lips. I kiss you.
Wake up, I tease. *Let me see
if your eyes are green today or blue.*
You beam your skeptical grin.
When it is time for me to leave,
car keys rattle in my hand.
You growl and clasp my arm close.
I promise to stay until you sleep.
Here at the end, I keep my vow.
You grip my hand,
so your nails cut my skin.
On both hands, I have narrow scabs.
I will have scars always.

This Night

Insomnia is a mountain and grief
is a lion ripping my throat.
I roar in my bed, terrified.
Did I think I would sleep undisturbed?
I walk room to room,
turn every light on in my house,
play Kitaro's Silk Road music,

and look at paintings on my walls.
Each frame draws attention to the scape.
Mountains rise. A road winds upward
and vanishes at the horizon.
Where is the path? I am lost
in a dense, hardwood forest, lost
in brushstokes of sunlight and shadow.

The man who lived ten months
with his eyes shut, died tonight
in a hospital bed. The artist is dead.
This night of his departure,
I will not sleep. I shall walk
among trees until I find the path,
until I reach the ascending road.

Carolina Bluebirds

This flock tells time.
They swoop into my yard
on December third and light
on the highest branches.
I know what they are up to.
Look how they stand still,
trying to pass for last leaves.
For a moment, I believe
they will stay until spring.
From branches of oaks,
they scope my birdhouses,
then glide down,
try each door. They do this
at the end of fall every year.
Every year, I am ready,
seed in the feeders. *Stay,* I whisper.
I need them to stay.
They don't care what I need.
They wing southward without a glance
like the loved one I tried to keep,
who at winter's approach flew forth
searching for the great haven.

Studying Winter

In Sapporo in February, soldiers
build cathedrals of ice
and shape elaborate figures
for the Festival of Snow.
I read about this with my students.
Each has photographs in a book,
a replica of St. Mary's Cathedral
fifty soldiers built with snow
and Gundam standing tall as a feed silo.

It's not winter, says the boy
who dips Skoal at break time
outside our portable classroom.

It ain't cold, he repeats with joy in his voice,
so we chuckle. It is April.
I know he will go home at three
to plant in his father's field.
Some time before dark I will plant
peas in my small garden.
The more Earth turns past solstice
the darker my morning
when I wake and dress and go to teach and to learn.
Cold will come the first week of January
as it always comes to Appalachia.
After summer, after fall,
winter shall come to these mountains.
An avalanche cannot stop itself.

Storm

It is too cold to stand looking out
but I do. I look through the picture
window into a white blizzard.
Pines snap and crash. They lie tangled
with downed power lines across my drive.

Birds flock to the front porch feeder
for seeds and crumbs;
birds I've watched, sparrow, nuthatch.
Through horizontal snow they fly,
chickadee, warbler, the bright

red cardinal with his mate, and others
not seen before at my feeder:
a fleck-breasted brown thrasher,
a purple finch, perfectly red,
and a blue jay singing distress.

Back in my dark hovel, I hover
near a kerosene heater that can
only knock the chill off one room.
It can only heat coffee to lukewarm.
I have a little food and a flashlight.

* * * *

I slept last night, sub-zero,
in two sets of clothes,
in a cap and coat and gloves.
Still bundled, I watch birds

fly from the hedge to the feeder.
They don't take tuns as they did.
Instead, they eat fast in a group
like a family seated around a table.

The phone is dead. I've known
isolation in the mountains, isolation
the norm, but now aloneness is stern,
my paneled den dark with gloom.

On the transistor radio
the local station is back,
broadcasting a sermon
when I want to hear what happened.

News from Atlanta and Chattanooga
is generic. In general: Storm of the Century,
from Florida to Canada,
tornados and blizzards,

mass power outage, 200 dead.
Hikers are lost somewhere
in the Blue Ridge. I am lost,
in my house, lost.

* * * *

Icicles hang from the eaves,
drip-freeze, an ice curtain as days pass.
I brave the cold, bring in snow
to melt for water and go out
in sunshine with birdseed.

I attack patches of ice
on my porch with a hoe and a sure hand
and start to shovel a path
to the mound shaped like my car.
My hands freeze as I free it
from its hull. It gleams. It starts
but won't budge. Cemented.

I look past the snow-weighted willow,
past debris, across the iced valley road.
There are no tracks. My heart locks.

* * * *

One squirrel joins the birds
on the porch to eat seeds.
Rain falls and fog fills the valley.
All I can see is my porch,
nothing beyond. Whiteout.

The house across the field has disappeared.
The power pole does not exist.
Birds fly in low under or between
icicles that hang sharp as swords.
The jay would bully, but today

with his long beak, he digs seeds
one by one and tosses them to small birds.
He takes one seed for himself,
then flies to the top branch of a maple.
I am the one who is growing impatient.

* * * *

On local radio *Party Line* I hear
how neighbor helps neighbor
here in Appalachia, how the
surefooted walk into deep coves
with portable heaters and fuel.

In my cave, I'm still in the dark
though I've learned there are things worse
than being all alone in a blizzard.
Fourteen more victims are listed. I know

their names, and names of the saved
who were rescued by sled from a mountain top
where power poles crashed through,
rescued from the house
of their dreams alive with wires.
The radio tells more than I want to hear.
One woman alone with her dead husband
since Friday is finally saved
this morning, his body recovered.

* * * *

Day six, I look out
past a flurry of hungry birds,
past trees bent with ice,
past my impassible drive,
across the white road.

No one is going to come here.
I stomp out the door onto the porch
kicking patches of ice with my boot toe.
With a broom handle, I demolish icicles
one by one. With a whack and a whack

I bring them down. Ice daggers
crash into boxwoods in a pileup.
Horrified birds fly from the hedge,
flee from my porch.
I hope they will come back.

Now in Another Land

Candide is young and naive.
He believes what he is told.
He heard Cunegonde, his true love,
was raped, disfigured, dead.

But no, she lives in a foreign land with
Don Issachar on Monday, Wednesday, Saturday,
She lives with the Grand Inquisitor
on Sunday, Tuesday, Thursday, Friday.

Candide pictures Cunegonde. He imagines her
young as on the day they kissed. When he
finds her somewhere else a second time,
she is ugly as a hag. He thinks

the eminent Professor Pangloss died
in battle. That never happened.
Pangloss is alive with syphilis,
his nose rotting, his teeth falling out.

Candide begins to trust only what he sees.
With his own eyes he sees Pangloss
hanging by the neck. Candide loses
faith in truth. He loses hope for

the best possible world. He stops staying
there is no effect without cause.
But, Pangloss did not die.
He lives even now in another land.

Music, Action, Voices

Music storms the stage.
Dense fog wafts left to right,
dissonant music and more dense fog.
Zeda enters. This is pure vision.
A trance longer than any on Earth.

She stumbles through a Stravinsky dream,
her coat ragged by strong wind.
Cacophony. Green mountains fade.
She trudges through deep snow.
There is one highway with many travelers.

The music is not in harmony with
the tenuous forms of children walking.
Now voices. *Where are we?*
Don't call me a refugee! Words
almost lost in the scream of violins.

Zeda wants to stop, wants to wake.
How do you stop such wickedness?
A stranger touches her arm, says *Hello,*
leads her in the dance. Center stage.
They leap like Balanchine's dancers.

The Property

How far have we walked?

I cannot judge.
Light on the snow blinds,
white reflected, white emphasized.

There is supposed to be a river.

I haven't seen it. All day
we walked on ice. I feel nothing.
I cannot feel the pain of my own feet.

Do you miss seeing trees?

Yes, I miss them. I no longer reason
as when we lived in the green world.
I'm intrigued by things we imagine.

You envision a moth free of its chrysalis.
I keep remembering myself, a boy
swimming naked in East River.

Look at these people.

So many. I thought no one lived here.
What is this place?
It is not on my map.

Do you think we are trespassing?

At the Gates

Attention travelers.
Step forward.
We are conducting
an investigation.
We want memory.
What did you see?
What did you hear?

Earth swallowed me
said the miner.
I burned on the stairs
said the fireman. I suffocated
said the meatpacker. My heart went bad
said the Shah. An assassin shot me
said the President. I died in the coup
said the Russian. I fell from the roof
said an addict. I froze on the mountain
said the Kurd. I died in the desert
said the American. I burned in my tank
said the Englishman. A bomb fell on my house
said the Libyan boy. I stopped breathing
cried an infant. I was beheaded
said the missionary. My captors hanged me
said the colonel. I died over Scotland
said a woman. I drowned at sea
said a Haitian. I died at the check point
said the policeman. I wanted sleep
said the insomniac. I died in my bed.
The ocean took me said the tourist.
The secretary said I was buried under rubble.
There was no cure said the nurse.

Ice in the Deep South

The oldest oak in the neighborhood fell last night,
crashed under the weight of ice,
and took to the ground our power lines.

On this bright day we gather to see
but can't bear to look at exposed roots,
can't stand the sound of chain saws

dismembering limbs all day, can't stomach
the sight of men at dusk, hauling the trunk away.
For a lifetime, this tree stood

as our landmark, our signal.
When you see the giant oak turn right.
How will anyone find us now?

My Father Told Me

He was at a Snapfinger Creek picnic,
eating his first peanut butter
when he first saw an airplane in the sky.
Age fifteen, absorbed
in the theory of light, I asked him,
"Is light electrons or waves?" If this
confused scientists for centuries,
why did Coach French want me to learn
the debate in six weeks? I couldn't see it.
As father told his story, I heard the engine
of the first plane to fly above Atlanta,
high, behind a far cloud.
At that time in my life, I wanted to probe
how the mind can travel fast as
the speed of flight, and how happy is the body
when the mind is somewhere else.
There are no photos from Snapfinger Creek,
but there is one shot of my young father,
radiant in the red glow of sunset.
This is no picnic. Show me the x-ray.
I can see it now. Light streams
as energy waves, flowing, healing the body.
I get it, but of course, I am older.

Looking for the Sons of My House

I am looking for the sons of my house,
grown from babies into boys,
three of them with dark brown eyes.
Where are they now? The one
who brought a snake down the hall
into my room. The one who
had to fall off the porch, to test every rule?
The young one who flew half-way
around the world to be my son?
Their bikes are wrecked, tossed
in the landfill with their outgrown shoes.
One day I saw they were no longer boys but men,
the one who drove me to night class in Asheville
when he was a teen, the same one
I stood with as mother of the groom.
Where are they now?
One whistles on a hillside, feeds his dogs.
One is stuck in rush-hour traffic, stuck
in a marriage I blessed. The young one
climbs today on a mountain in Switzerland.
All of them far from the mother house.

Recovery

Scars on his body say something was taken.
This is the nightmare he dreams
years later in the hospital. A nurse
scrubs blood from what's left of his leg.
Roses in a vase turn brown when he sits
on the chair. They blacken, smell rank in three days.
"God," he swears at the wall.
Long time passing, contempt is saved.
He braces himself. A therapist forces him
to stand, makes him walk in the hall.
Something remains and it grows, like guilt
after bombing, like a soldier's after-thought.

Walking Around Lake Knowles with Sarah

The plan was to turn left
at the corner, go home,
but I took her hand,
went right instead because
there was a turtle in distress.

The turtle was large,
with a scarred shell
and seemed confused,
moving from the sidewalk
into rush-hour traffic.

I said "Mother Earth is calling,"
and my granddaughter, not five,
believed and followed me.
She asked, *How did you hear
Mother Earth calling?*

The turtle pulled in its head.
I said, *I didn't hear with my ears.*
Uh huh, Sarah nodded. She spoke
the way one speaks to a pet,
said, *Come out.*

The turtle stuck out its head.
I turned it toward the lake.
It left the sidewalk,
slid across the grass, down the bank,
and splashed with gusto into the water.

We cheered. I said, *Turtles
are old, best-loved creatures.*
Shhhh, Sarah hissed, said, *I know.*
We walked a second time
around Lake Knowles, then home.

Figments

White light moves
in my dark room. It looks like
when I press my eyelids closed
at the end of day, then see

gloss that blurs truth.
I shift in bed, turn
and turn, unable to sleep.
Sheen moves across the floor,

to the door into the hall.
It hovers and glows.
My thoughts go off center.
I turn, waiting for morning.

I am staying here
in Brunswick, Georgia
in a white Victorian house
with its wide porch across from

a park Oglethorpe planned
when 300 year-old oaks
were saplings rising
at the edge of the marsh.

Something tells me not to go
too far back, only stay
till I find the ghost woman and man,
lovers who haunt this house.

Friday I found his blue suit
hanging in the closet. I found
a frilled dog-winkle sea shell
on the nightstand in my room.

Saturday, in a milk glass bud vase
on the dresser, a rose appeared.
I pressed it between
the pages of my book.

The house is quiet today.
Maybe she has gone for a walk
in the neighborhood. A dog barks
a genteel bark. Neighbors look out

their front-room windows.
Is that her sitting in the park
under the moss-festooned oak?
When I approach, there is no one.

Arriving Late

for Dorothy Simpson Weatherford

I win the argument. Why don't you concede?
You wanted to leave at five a.m.
I said *Turn east. See the ocean.*
God knows if we will come back.
At the mention of God, you drove across
the causeway, away from home.

We arrived in time to see the sun rise
over the Atlantic, walked, tried to stand
inside the circle the sun made
on the shore, got our feet wet,
got sand in our shoes. You tried not
to show how much it pleased you.

The drive home from the coast to the mountains
is always hard on the body. Remember
we arrived one hour later than we would have
at the clean-up scene of a wreck. A transfer truck
crashed head on, killing two sisters who left
the coast at five o'clock this morning.

Women Walking Around

Women walk around the town square,
women alone,
not one of them young,
at the courthouse paying taxes,
at the post office getting their mail,
one coming from the library
with a book tucked under her arm.

I am one of them, stepping through life,
despite my sister's fall, her death.
Dorothy, buried yesterday at Westview.
Myself, wanting not to think how when men
took our chairs away from the grave site
and rolled back the green carpet
I saw the graves

of my mother, my father,
Grandmother, Grandfather,
the graves of another sister, a brother.
Dorothy is with them, while I walk
among the women of my town,
paying bills, not one man in sight
except for those behind counters

selling us stamps, stamping
the electric bill *Paid,*
the clerk in the drug store
selling wrinkle cream.
Women coiffed,
step from the beauty shop—
sisters I have never met.

Teaching Myself
How to Burn Last Year's Leaves

If you live in a forest,
don't burn on a windy day.
Look on the boundary oak
for the surveyor's orange ribbon.
If it's not dancing, if it dangles,
you can hope burning is safe.
Best, burn when rain is predicted.

Rake leaves onto the dirt driveway.
Make small leaf mounds.
Burn one or two leaf piles at a time.
Don't let yourself think of the day
your young sons scorched the mountainside.
Do not look across the drive
where your old home place used to be.

Forget it. The cabin was dismantled,
bulldozed to the ground, buried.
Don't think of the man who found you
burning leaves one spring and said,
Let me help you. Rake and burn
leaf piles 3 & 4, 5 & 6.

Let sudden wind frighten. Rake faster
when you hear thunder. Rake hot coals
into the gravel.
              Stop only when rain
drives you back to the tool shed.
Tomorrow you will see bright green foliage
of five thousand day lilies lining your drive,
promising to bloom.

What She Saw and What She Heard

On the mountain a woman saw
the road bank caved in
from winter's freeze-thaw
and April rain erosion.

Trees leaned over the road the way
strands of hair hung on her forehead.
She gaped, her face as tortured
as the face she saw engraved in dirt.

Roots growing sideways shaped brows,
two eyes. Humus washed
down the bank like a nose.
Lower down, where a rock

was shoved out by weathering,
a hole formed the shape of a mouth.
The woman groaned, *Agh!*
Her spirit toppled

to the ground, slithered
under the roots of an oak.
She stood there asking
What? Who?

Back to reason, back home
she finished her questions:
What can one make of the vision, that face
on the north side of the mountain?

Reckoning comes, a thought:
It is not the image of a witch nor a god,
but Earth's face, mouth open saying,
Save me.

"No Good Thing Ever Dies"

(Last words from *Shawshank Redemption*)

A vicious wind rips leaves,
takes them down.
I wrap my cardigan close, frown,
and brood, changed again in my life.

Where else can I live
with only two brown months,
still have dogwoods in spring,
purple verbena and yellow zinnias until frost,

and have the psychedelia of fall
flashing red-orange on my mountainsides?
I wrap my cardigan close.
There is no elsewhere for me.

Life changes before we are born,
while we live, and after we die.
Everything changes, yet for eons
we've had Father, The Good Mother.

Back to the beginning to time,
at every place on our planet, family exists.
I sit near the hearth. I keep truth,
I keep love and hope no good thing ever dies.

Green Place

It-se-yi: fresh, green place
stretches from Brasstown Bald Mountain
to Brasstown village in North Carolina,
the old home of Chief Settawiga.

From Brasstown Bald Mountain in Georgia,
Cherokee people walked
to the home of Settawiga,
led by federal troops.

Cherokee People walked
through cold rain and snow,
led by federal troops
on The Trail of Tears.

Through cold rain and snow,
they cried for *It-se-yi*, not *Unt-se-yi*
on their Trail of Tears.
Truth was lost in translation.

They cried for *It-se-yi*, not *Unt-se-yi*.
The scholar was mistaken,
truth lost in his translation.
It is not the place where there is brass.

The scholar was mistaken
Settawiga taught his people, saying:
It is not the place where there is brass
that we carry in us as we go.

Settawiga led his people to Oklahoma
teaching them, saying:
We carry in us
It-se-yi, *Green Place.*

Ghost of Candide

for Bettie M. Sellers

It was the wrong time to meet
a lost relative-by-marriage
but we met. We walked
on the red dirt road
in the forest, her best world.

I am not married to your cousin anymore,
she said. *The divorce is final.*
I thought I saw the end in lines
across her face. It was the sun
playing artist, using a twig

of a sapling for a brush, painting
random shadows on her cheek.
White petals fell, dropped
by the change of a season.
She never noticed petals falling,

instead, turned and pointed
to pink buds of laurel. Even now
when I walk there, I feel
the presence of a persistent spirit.
I won't die from it, she said.

In the Deep End

Wrapped in warm water,
I feel no pain, not even when
I bend my pool noodle and pretend
to ride a bike for one hour,
no pain when I bounce on a non-existing
trampoline, rising high into the air
with each kick and jump.
Glass walls around this cocoon,
keep me inside, keep me
counting blue tiles at poolside.

On this fall day, my legs bear weight,
my soul bears witness, slipping out
through my eyes, to life
on the other side, to one maple tree,
leaf by leaf, turning golden.
Focus on the golden tree,
I whisper to myself,
turning my back on bent pines.
Focus, I say, not letting myself look
at other trees that have already gone blank.

The Skin Diver's Memory

Beneath the killing sea
that holds a wealth of secrets,
off the shore of Morehead City,
a German 352 U-boat

with its own rich secrets
is an island of plenty.
The German U-boat
is a living reef,

a plentiful island, submersed.
I've been there. I've seen it,
a living reef where creatures
of the deep make a home.

I've been there. I've seen it,
a torpedo, its mouth crusted,
make a home of the deep
on this deserted battlefield.

I look into the crusted mouth
of a torpedo forgotten
on a deserted battlefield
known as Torpedo Alley.

A torpedo, forgotten,
is the Heaven for Angelfish.
In Torpedo Alley one day
an angel swam out through the mouth,

out of the Heaven for Angelfish.
It brushed my cheek with its fin.
A fish swam out of a torpedo
and I understood then underwater

the chemistry of a U-boat, the slow
transfiguration from evil to good
off the shore of Morehead City
beneath the killing sea.

Transplanting

At an abandoned house site, edge of the woods,
lies a patch of periwinkle ground cover:
glossy green leaves, violet flowers,
a thick carpet spread across the forest floor.

I've come here at times to dig squares
so now periwinkle covers my side yard. It holds
banks of the mountain road near my cabin.
Imagine. All the vinca I will ever need.

My adopted son has forgotten Vietnam, war.
He wants his own forest, so he bought and planted
four sunset maples, two sugar maples, five dogwoods,
one redbud, and eight rhododendron shrubs

in his one-third acre Atlanta yard.
"It's a start," he said when he called, and I laughed
when he came home to the mountains this morning.
He's here on the business he's building

from the ground up, that forest in his backyard.
We walk to the patch with boxes and a shovel.
I watch as he works with commitment. He digs
a cluster of green, gently lifts each clump,

places it in a box. He takes one clump
and another, none from the same spot.
He digs, lifts, places, moves, and digs.
When he has all he can carry, he stops,

goes back to each dig site. He looks at small wounds,
stretches a tendril across soil, pats it down,
then looks up and asks me, *What do you think?*
I tell him, *Your vinca will thrive.*

Living Above the Frost Line

Leaves fall and windows open
to mountain ridges hidden all summer.
'Frost line' is not definitive, but I discuss it
with old-timers who believe and say,
Grow apples. Up here on the mountain
the life of my elephant ear plant
gets extended a few days. This green fan
cannot thrive, according to experts,
but it stands its ground. The growth season ended.
Mid-November and I don't know what to believe.
Nothing is certain except death.
I pay taxes but can't count on the state
to give one load of gravel for my road
used by travelers since 1830.
Living above the frost line I get a slanted view.
Cleome still blooms, but time is running out.
I must take into account the coming of the hard freeze,
must cover my dahlia with pine straw.
Along the mulched path, it's clear
experts are wrong. Red nasturtiums bloom.
Here in my garden
knockout roses still bloom their hearts out.

The text of the book is typeset in 10-point Minion.
The book was designed by Lesley Landis Designs
and printed by United Graphics.